Anthony Burns Elem. School
Library Media Center
60 Gallery Road
Stafford, VA 22554

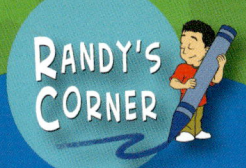

Randy's Corner

DAY BY DAY WITH...
SELENA GOMEZ

BY TAMRA ORR

Mitchell Lane
PUBLISHERS

P.O. Box 196
Hockessin, Delaware 19707
Visit us on the web: www.mitchelllane.com
Comments? email us:
mitchelllane@mitchelllane.com

Copyright © 2012 by Mitchell Lane Publishers. All rights reserved. No part of this book may be reproduced without written permission from the publisher. Printed and bound in the United States of America.

Printing   1   2   3   4   5   6   7   8   9

RANDY'S CORNER

DAY BY DAY WITH...

Beyoncé
Dwayne "The Rock" Johnson
Eli Manning
Justin Bieber
LeBron James

Miley Cyrus
Selena Gomez
Shaun White
Taylor Swift
Willow Smith

Library of Congress Cataloging-in-Publication Data
Orr, Tamra.
 Day by day with Selena Gomez / by Tamra Orr.
   p. cm. — (Randy's corner)
 Includes bibliographical references and index.
 ISBN 978-1-58415-987-2 (library bound)
 1. Gomez, Selena, 1992– —Juvenile literature. 2. Actors—United States—Biography—Juvenile literature. 3. Singers—United States—Biography—Juvenile literature. I. Title.
 PN2287.G585O77 2011
 792.02'8092—dc22
 [B]
                                                                                       2011006176

eBook ISBN: 9781612281551

ABOUT THE AUTHOR: Tamra Orr is a full-time author living in the Pacific Northwest with her family. She has written over 250 books for kids of all ages, including celebrity biographies for Mitchell Lane Publishers (*Shia LaBeouf*, *Brenda Song*, *Robert Pattinson*, *Jordin Sparks* and *Justin Bieber*). Orr loves reading all kinds of books, plus writing letters to friends across the globe.

PUBLISHER'S NOTE: The following story has been thoroughly researched, and to the best of our knowledge represents a true story. While every possible effort has been made to ensure accuracy, the publisher will not assume liability for damages caused by inaccuracies in the data and makes no warranty on the accuracy of the information contained herein. This story has not been authorized or endorsed by Selena Gomez.

PLB

DAY BY DAY WITH

SELENA GOMEZ

You may know Selena Gomez from seeing her on TV or in movies. She loves to act! You may also know her music. She sang "Cruella de Vil" for Disney's movie *101 Dalmatians*. She has even been in the Jonas Brothers' music video for their single, "Burnin' Up."

Selena Marie Gomez was born on July 22, 1992, in New York City. Her parents, Amanda Cornett and Ricardo Gomez, divorced when she was five. She and her mother moved to Grand Prairie, Texas, to be closer to her mother's family.

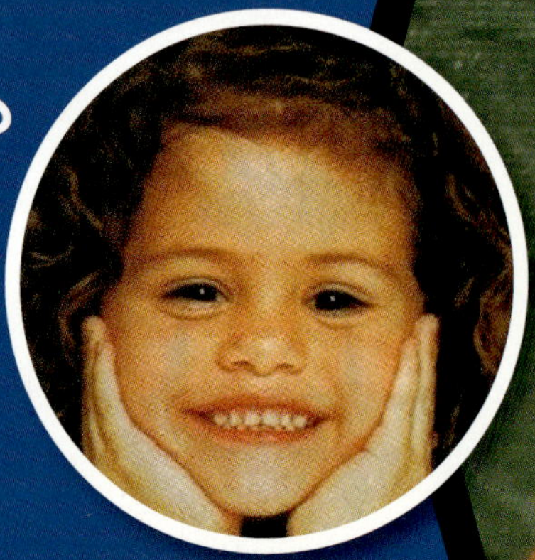

SELENA AS A KID

SELENA WITH HER DOG

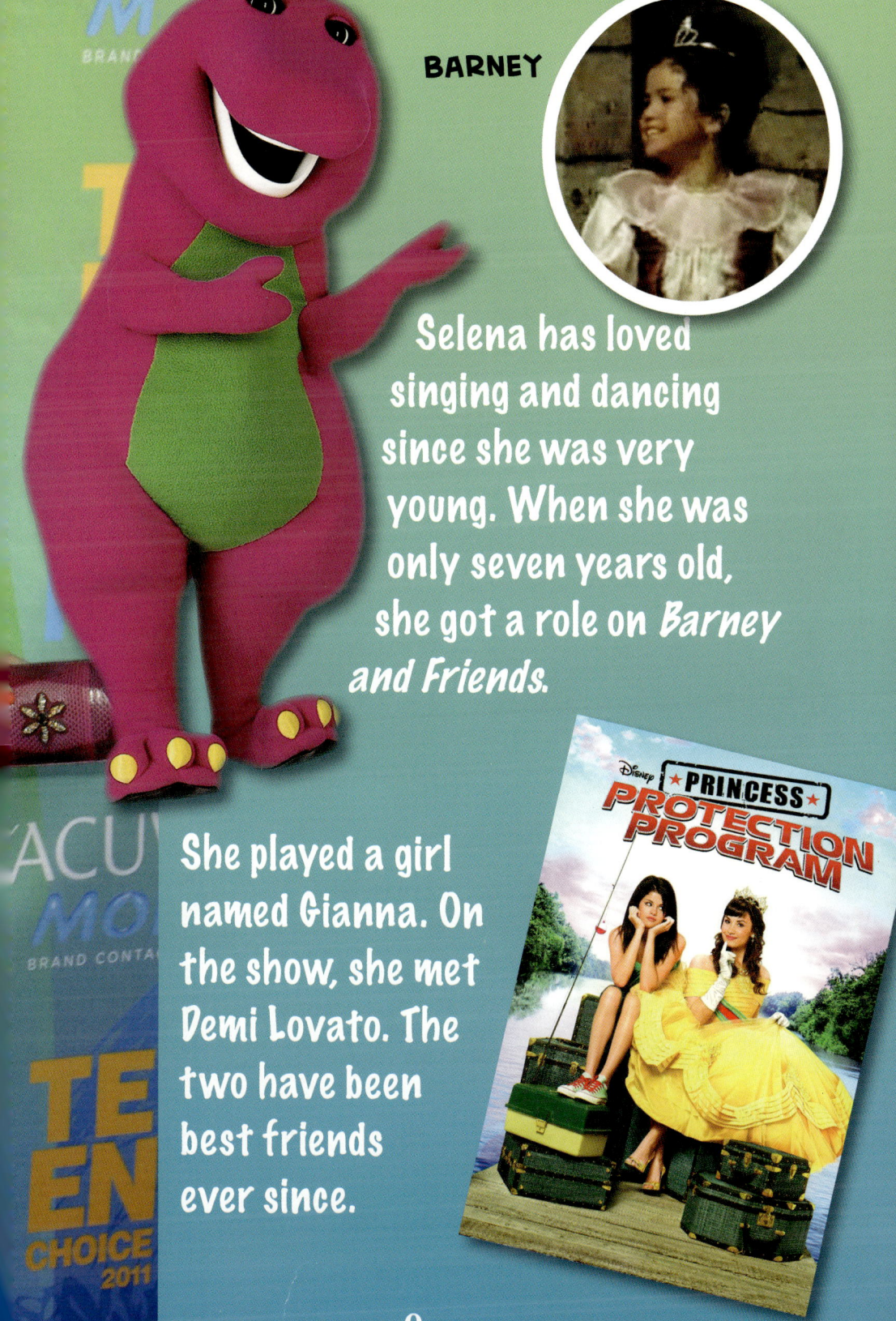

BARNEY

Selena has loved singing and dancing since she was very young. When she was only seven years old, she got a role on *Barney and Friends*.

She played a girl named Gianna. On the show, she met Demi Lovato. The two have been best friends ever since.

Just like other young people, Selena loves stopping by to say hi to Mickey Mouse at Walt Disney World. She has made many hits with Disney.

PIZZA IS SELENA'S FAVORITE FOOD, AND CHEESECAKE IS HER FAVORITE DESSERT

Selena enjoys hanging out with her TV family from *Wizards of Waverly Place.* She is close to David Henrie and Jake T. Austin, her brothers on the show. "They basically ARE my brothers," she says. "They're my real family. I don't have any real-life siblings, so this way I can have brothers."

MARIA CANALS-BARRERA & DAVID DELUISE

JENNIFER STONE & DAVID HENRIE

Whether going to birthday parties in wild costumes or learning how to surf in the ocean, Selena loves keeping busy. "Once you ride that first wave," she says, "there's something about it that keeps you riding more and more."

Selena tries to balance her time between acting and singing. Along with years of performing as Alex Russo on *Wizards of Waverly Place*—and even in the movie—she is in the 2011 movie *The Muppets*. She also performs concerts across the country.

One of Selena's best friends is singer Taylor Swift. Selena often goes to her friend for advice. "She gives the most thought-out answers," says Selena. "We literally talk every day."

Selena not only hangs out with friends, but she also likes to spend time making music with her band, Selena Gomez and the Scene. The group released the single "A Year without Rain" on the album *Kiss and Tell*. The group gets along great and Selena says, "I like having people with me to lean on, and people to write with and have fun with."

When Selena isn't singing or acting, she likes to help others. In 2008, she was named spokesperson for UNICEF. She travels to exotic places like Ghana in Africa to discover how people live there. She also helps raise money for children in need.

Promoting her shows, movies, and music takes up a lot of Selena's time. She often appears on shows to be interviewed. That can be fun too... like when she ate Ben and Jerry's ice cream with Jimmy Fallon.

KLOE & KOURTNEY KARDASHIAN

Wearing pretty clothes and the latest fashions is another part of Selena's life. She attends fashion shows to keep up on the newest trends. Of course, she also likes casual clothes. She says she has 20 pairs of sneakers in all different colors in her closet.

Becoming famous at such a young age has taught Selena a lot about growing up. Her advice to other young people is, "You can't

think that you're not as good as anyone else. Be careful of what you do and say and who you hang out with. Represent yourself well."

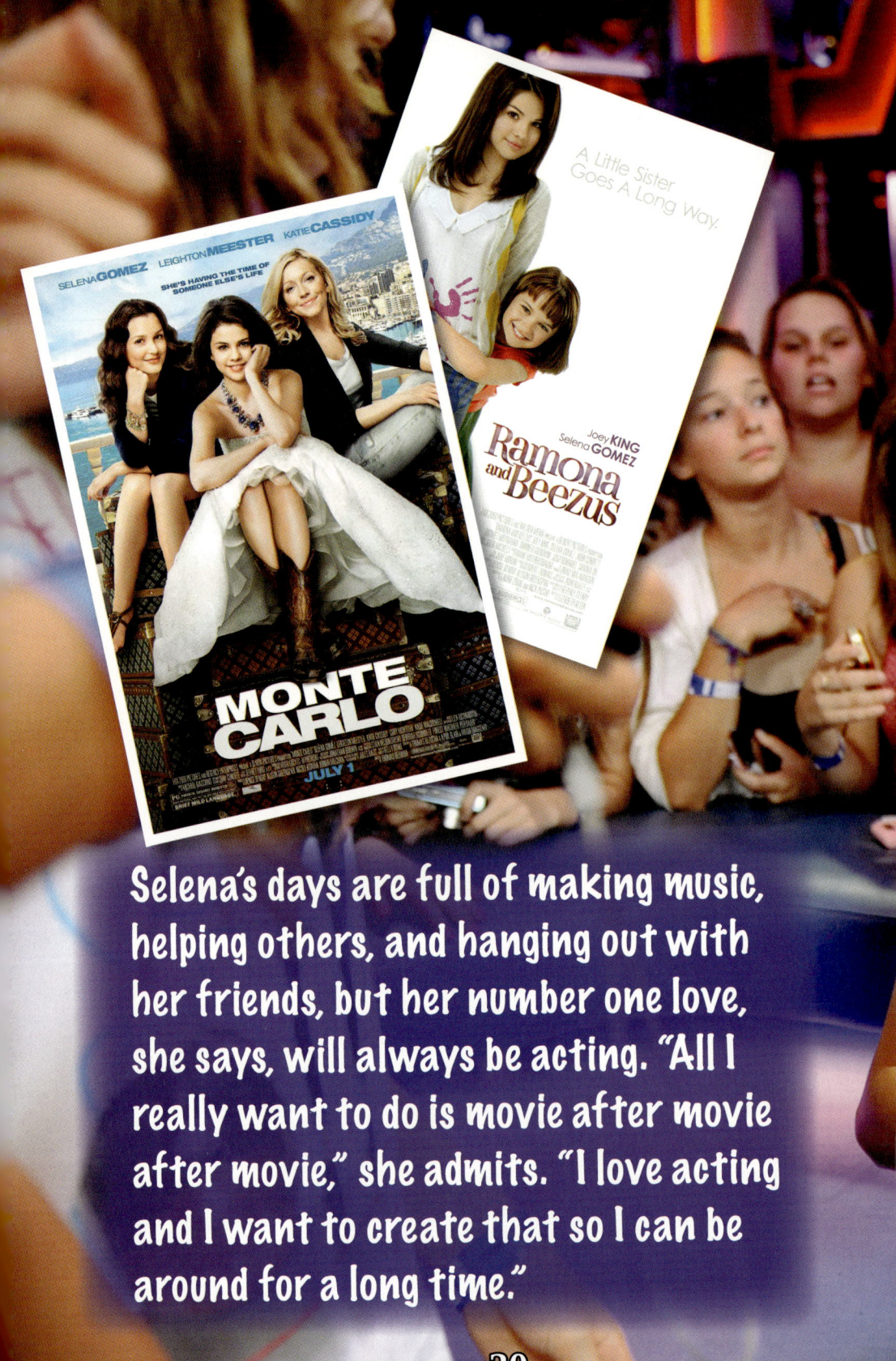

Selena's days are full of making music, helping others, and hanging out with her friends, but her number one love, she says, will always be acting. "All I really want to do is movie after movie after movie," she admits. "I love acting and I want to create that so I can be around for a long time."

FURTHER READING

Books
If you enjoyed this book about Selena Gomez, you might also like these other books from Mitchell Lane Publishers:
Day By Day with Miley Cyrus, by Amie Jane Leavitt
Day By Day with Taylor Swift, by Kayleen Reusser
Selena Gomez, by Kayleen Reusser.

On the Internet
Demi Lovato Official Site
http://demilovato.com/
Selena Gomez Official Site
http://selenagomez.com/
Taylor Swift Official Site
http://www.taylorswift.com/

Works Consulted
Bartolomeo, Joey. "Boy Wonder." *People*, April 19, 2010, Vol. 73, Issue 15.
"It's My Life: Selena Gomez." *PBS Kids*. November 2007. http://pbskids.org/itsmylife/celebs/interviews/selena.html
Rosenberg, Carissa. "When It Comes to Guy Drama and Girl Crimes, Selena Has It All Figured Out." *Seventeen Magazine*, 2011. http://www.seventeen.com/entertainment/features/selena-gomez-interview
"Selena Gomez." *Bio: The True Story* (A&E Network). 2011. http://www.biography.com/articles/Selena-Gomez-504530

INDEX

101 Dalmatians 4
Africa 23
Austin, Jake T. 12, 13
Barney and Friends 9
Canals-Barrera, Maria 12
Cornett, Amanda (mother) 6, 7
DeLuise, David 12
Disney 4, 11
Fallon, Jimmy 25
Gomez, Ricardo (father) 6
Gomez, Selena
  acting 16, 30
  band 20
  birth 6
  charity 23, 30
  fashion 15, 16, 26–27
favorite foods 11
musical career 16, 20–21
playing Gianna 9
surfing 15
UNICEF spokesperson 23
Greene, Ashley 19
Henrie, David 12, 13
Jonas Brothers 4
Kardashians 26–27
Kiss and Tell 20, 21
Lovato, Demi 8, 9
Muppets, The 16
Selena Gomez and the Scene 20–21
Stone, Jennifer 12
Swift, Taylor 18, 19
Wizards of Waverly Place 12, 16

PHOTO CREDITS: Cover design—Joe Rasemas; p. 3—Michael Germana/Globe Photos, Inc; pp. 4–5, 18–19—Kevin Mazur/TCA 2011/Getty Images; pp. 6–7—Michael Tran/FilmMagic; p. 8—D. Long/Globe Photos, Inc; pp. 10–11—AP Photo/Disney, Garth Vaughan; pp. 12–13—Kevin Mazur/TCA 2010/Getty Images; p. 14—Gregg DeGuire/PictureGroup via AP Images; pp. 16–17—Paul Hiffmeyer/Disney via Getty Images; pp. 20–21—Angel Weiss/Getty Images; pp. 22–23—Lisa Lake/WireImage for Children's Hospital of Philadelphia; p. 23—Michael Buckner/Getty Images for OfficeMax; pp. 24–25—Theo Wargo/Getty Images; pp. 26–27—John Parra/WireImage; pp. 28–29—Gustavo Caballero/Getty Images; pp. 30–31—AP Photo/Arthur Mola. All other photos—CreativeCommons. Every effort has been made to locate all copyright holders of materials used in this book. Any errors or omissions will be corrected in future editions of the book.